The Power of Effective Time Management

The 9 Strategies To "Get IT Done"

Hasheem Francis & Deborah Francis

The Power of Effective Time Management
Authors: Hasheem Francis & Deborah Francis
Cover design by: BTP Marketing Group
Edited by: Spirit of Excellence Writing & Editing Services
ISBN: 978-0692546642
Published by: BTP Publishing Group, Plymouth, FL (www.BTPPublish.com)

BTP
Publishing Group
WHERE LEADERS HAVE A VOICE

Table of Contents

INTRODUCTION

One of the most common complaints in today's world is that we are just too busy to find time for the things that really matter. We are so consumed by our work and then by our responsibilities for our family and society that we get little time for personal enrichment of any kind. We do not find time to pursue our passion.

However, if we managed things in a better way, we could be able to find time for the things that we like to do. It is all about proper management.

There are so many distractions in today's world of business that few people manage their time effectively. Cell phones, social media, emails, RSS news feeds, the Internet, online meetings, software updates, conference calls, text messaging, and online bill pay, all created to make our work more productive, can make time much less manageable if not used wisely.

As people cram more activities into their personal lives, scheduling, managing, and prioritizing tasks have become even more critical.

There is a broad difference between quantity and quality when it comes to managing the use of our time. Few leaders spend a fraction of time managing their own time compared to watching the activity of their employees' time. A common mistake many people make is that they go about their day without any direction or focus. Then others try to stuff in too many things for the day and end up feeling disappointed because they have not accomplished anything.

In this book, you will find strategies you can implement that will help you maximize your time. Imagine the feeling at the end of the day, knowing you accomplished everything you set out to do and made the best use of your time.

Imagine having a plan for each day that actually works! Imagine being aware of all the distractions and learning how to avoid them.

This book will give you the strategies and tools you need to effectively manage your time and get the fulfillment and satisfaction from knowing you got the most out of each day.

Chapter 1
THE POWER OF GETTING MORE OUT OF YOUR TIME

Have you ever heard someone say, "I wish I had more time in the day"? When was the last time you heard this? Were you the one who said it? We all run from task to task and event to event at light speed, trying to find ways to do and accomplish more.

Don't we all wish we could maximize the effectiveness of every minute we spend? In order to do that, it is critically important to identify the time-wasting habits in our lives—those little seemingly harmless activities that are actually sucking time from us without our knowledge. These are the activities that cause you to wonder at the end of the day, "Where has all my time gone?"

"My general attitude to life is to enjoy every minute of every day. I never do anything with a feeling of, Oh God, I've got to do this today." **- Richard Branson**

Some people seem to accomplish far more than others in their day, week, month, and lifetime. Richard Branson is the founder of the Virgin Group, which comprises more than 400 companies. His accomplishments are astounding. He started Virgin as a mail order record business. Today, Virgin is one of the top companies in the world. Richard also created a non-profit entrepreneurial foundation called Virgin Unite, which focuses on entrepreneurial approaches to social and environmental issues.

With all of Richard Branson's accomplishments how does he find the time to Get It Done? The good news is there is no more time! You may be thinking "How can that be good news?"

In this respect, the playing field is level:
   ✓ Everyone gets the same 24 hours in a day.

✓ Your competition does not have more hours in a day than you.
✓ The richest man cannot buy even one more minute of time in a day!
✓ You can only manage yourself and activities more effectively.

Answer this question: How many hours are there in a week? If you answered 40 hours, more than likely, you work a 9 to 5 job with the weekends off. If you answered 168 hours, more than likely, you're an entrepreneur or you're just great at multiplication (24 hours' x 7 days = 168 hours).

Many people believe that there are only 8 "working" hours in a day, but we all know there are 24 hours in a day. Everyone has the same 24 hours whether you work a 9 to 5 job or you're an entrepreneur. There is simply no exception. Then why is it that some people manage to accomplish so much in those 24 hours while some simply waste their time away? Have you ever felt like the day just flew by and you had accomplished nothing on your so-called "to do list"?

Since there is no way to make a day last more than 24 hours, the next best thing we can do is maximize our efficiency during those twenty-four hours.

Having a "Get It Done" list instead of a "To Do" list gives you a sense of direction and lets you know exactly what it is you are supposed to get done for that day.

A "Get It Done" list should only have 3 to 5 "important" things that must get done. I like to call it my 3 to 5 income-producing activities, and mowing the lawn is not one of them. You have to determine what's important to you and "Get It Done."

Your time is an asset. Decide what you want to do with your time each day and invest it wisely. Are you going to enrich yourself in some way? You may be planning to do something creative or just become more productive. When you know what you want and you are willing to go after it, you begin to view your time as an asset.

Blocking out a set time that you can create a "Get It Done" list is very effective. This can be done in the morning while everyone is still sleeping, or in the evening right before you go to bed. It is very important that you are not distracted during this time. It allows you to set how much time you should invest on each individual activity, and the sense of urgency and lack of distractions prevents your mind from wandering and improves your focus.

The power of focusing on one thing at a time is of the utmost importance and ties in with the rest of the points.

While multi-tasking is a common activity in today's fast-paced world, we must be realistic and realize that many items cannot be grouped together and done simultaneously. Focusing on one thing at a time not only allows you to maintain full concentration on that one activity so you can complete it efficiently, it also results in a high quality of work as your attention is not diverted to other issues.

Workaholics often have this thinking that giving yourself a break is being too indulgent and is something to be avoided at all costs. I can relate to this—I would work, work, work and at the end of the day, I would realize I did not take any time out for me. So, I would stay up later and try to find time to read or watch something I enjoy just to take my mind off the next project. The truth is that this was detrimental to my health and it also zapped my creative energy. I was doing my life, family, and business a huge disservice by not investing any time for myself.

In short, an occasional break or reward for yourself is essential to continue to function effectively. Learn to be selfish with your "me" time. When you are spending the better part of your day at work and a significant amount of time each day performing your various other obligations, schedule at least an hour every day for your personal development. Remember that improving self is extremely vital.

Setting goals is somewhat similar to writing a "Get It Done" list. The difference is that your goals provide a big picture view of your objectives. Your goals should be classified into short-term and long-term goals for a clearer picture of what you plan to achieve. Your "Get It Done" list is the stepping stone to accomplishing the big picture.

If you diligently take action and implement the given strategies in this book, you will be well on your way to maximizing your efficiency and having a renewed sense of vigor in carrying out your daily activities!

For those who work a typical 40-hour work week, it is estimated that the average person spends:

- ✓ 2.5 hours per day surfing the Internet
- ✓ 1.5 hours per day text messaging
- ✓ 1.5 hours per day reading emails
- ✓ 4 hours per day watching T.V.

That is a total of 9.5 hours of precious time wasted.

PRODUCTION

MY TIME IS AN ASSET

DISTRACTIONS

When people are asked why they are not organized, the number one reason given is: "I don't have the time." The fact is, people choose to be disorganized and this is due to the "Procrastination Monster."

Procrastination is a monster that lurks in the lives of every single person. It is the enemy of productivity, the number one cause of lost opportunities, and the ultimate killer of momentum.

Therefore, to be able to effectively control your activities and make every second count, it is vital for you to slay that Procrastination Monster!

Like all other important activities worth doing in life, slaying the Procrastination Monster is something that requires a huge amount of discipline and focus, especially at the start of your day. The master key to doing that, however, is pretty simple: start the day doing the activity you dread most.

The rationale behind this method is that once you are done with the most dreaded activity, you would feel such a sense of accomplishment and invincibility that you know nothing else can stop you. You will also gain a huge amount of momentum that will leave you rolling over the rest of your daily activities without delay.

Instead of slaying many Procrastination Monsters all throughout the day, all you have to do is to slay the king at the start of the day and the rest of the minions will automatically diminish in power, or even disappear altogether, making your day much more productive with a much clearer sense of direction and focus.

Do not underestimate the power of this skill due to its simplicity. Simplicity is where beauty resides! Once you start getting the feel of how to slay that Procrastination Monster, you will start shaving hours off unwanted shuffling and deliberating, and finally start getting things done in the fastest and most effective manner!

Effectively managing priorities is about behavioral change. We need to learn how to invest more time acting instead of reacting. The skills described herein will help you become better organized and manage time more effectively which will increase productivity, but only if you adapt the behavioral changes as outlined throughout this book.

The fact that most people never really invested in a time management program suggests that they do not feel that this is an issue that needs to be addressed. You are different, because you are a leader.

When poor organizational skills lead to wasted time, this time cannot be retrieved. Every leader needs to evaluate where their time is going on any given day and then implement a few time saving methods to overcome their biggest time wasters. Implementation of too many techniques at one time can result in spending more time organizing than working, or becoming overwhelmed and just returning to old ways out of frustration.

There are numerous time wasters; indecision and procrastination are perhaps the two biggest offenders. However, they are closely followed by inefficiency, interruptions, unnecessary errors, crisis management, poor organization, ineffective meetings, micro-managing, failure to delegate, and lack of policies, procedures, or standards to be followed.

According to several studies, the average person experiences 40 to 50 interruptions a day that take about 5 minutes each. This means that we spend over 4 hours each day dealing with unplanned events. Until you value yourself, you won't value your time. Until you value your time, you will not do anything with it.

What is the value of your time? It seems like there would be a simple answer but if you are using how much money you make as your yardstick and dividing it by a unit measure of time, maybe an hour, you could be dramatically undervaluing your time.

Instead of placing a value on your time, try valuing each task you perform.

Chapter 2
THE POWER OF TIME

As the saying goes, "time is money" and in fact, oftentimes, time is actually more important than money. You can certainly make use of time intelligently to make back money you've lost, but even if you have the wealth of Bill Gates, a second lost is a second lost. There is simply no way you can buy back lost time. It is really clear that the most precious resource we all have is time.

"Time is more value than money. You can get more money, but you cannot get more time." – **Jim Rohn**

This brings us to the topic of knowing the importance and power of time. Have you caught yourself thinking, "If only I had just one more hour every day to do what I want to do"?

There are certain time wasting activities that you may be involved in that will cause you to wonder at the end of the day, where has all my time gone?

The first step to correcting your time wasting habits, like all bad habits, is to identify where you have gone wrong. To that end, I urge you to try out this little experiment.

We have provided a time chart for you on the following page, or you can design your own. The goal is to evaluate how your time is being invested. The experiment starts at the beginning of every hour or at intervals that better fit your schedule. Insert what you have done for the past hour.

Don't let the fear of the time it will take to accomplish something stand in the way of you doing it. The time will pass anyway; we might just as well put that passing time to the best possible use.

Daily Activity	Time Invested	Total

Make this time log as detailed as possible, indicating exactly how many minutes you spend on each activity in the day. At the end of the day, evaluate your chart and you will be amazed at how much time you actually spend on non-productive activities.

You will realize how much time you spend on checking your emails, daydreaming, taking unnecessary phone calls, shopping on the Internet, updating your social media status, deciding what to eat for lunch, and a plethora of other non-productive activities. At the time of writing this paragraph, my phone is vibrating letting me know I have an incoming email. I know if I take my focus off what I am currently doing, it can cost me valuable time.

The steps to bringing discipline to your life are similar to growing a business—both require consistent focus.

"I don't focus on what I'm up against. I focus on my goals and I try to ignore the rest." – **Venus Williams**

One cannot achieve success in being disciplined overnight. Many people try using overnight methods and fail miserably and out of frustration, return back to their undisciplined life. It takes time to develop discipline.

You can think of time as the ultimate management of your life: Time = Life. Therefore, either you waste your time and waste of your life, or you master your time and master your life. Time never stops; it keeps on flowing. All you can do is utilize that flowing time effectively.

Many people wander through life making excuses. Anytime a procrastinator sees something as complicated, they will frequently make excuses why they can't deal with the issue. If you desire to better your life, you must develop the "Get It Done" attitude: Whatever tries to block me from my accomplishments, I will break through it.

Are you ascertaining that no matter how hard you try, you are not accomplishing your goals? Are you ready to enjoy your life, a successful career, a healthy and fit body, and a loving relationship? Do you know what it would take to accomplish these things? An investment of TIME.

Now look towards the ground and notice if there are any chains holding you down, stopping you from being free to accomplish your dreams. In order to succeed, you have to overcome not only your fear of failure, but your fear of success.

You may be as shocked as I was when I first heard that some people suffered from the fear of success. It looks illogical to push aside the very things we want. We are unique, but our problems are not.

The "Seven Fears" you must overcome if you want to succeed:

1. Fear of the unidentified. "I don't know what it would be like to be in a loving relationship or successful career."

2. Fear that success doesn't fit your self-image. "What is an average girl from the Bronx doing sitting at the table with Fortune 500 CEOs?"

3. Fear that people will not like you if you are successful. "If I'm successful in my business, people are going to say that my success changed me."

4. Fear that you don't merit success. "Who am I to think I can be successful?"

5. Fear that success has a scary consequence. "If my business gets too big, I won't have enough time to spend with my family."

6. Fear that your parents won't love you if you are more successful than they are. "I don't want my parents to feel bad."

7. Fear that to be successful is to fulfill your parents' wishes. "I'm angry at them for not showing me enough attention when I was a kid. I'll show them—I won't pursue a successful career."

If you have the power to dream, you can design your vision to meet your destination. Think of how you are and how you desire your future to be. You can create a vision to bring in power and success to your life, and it can also work for your career, your relationships, and health. When you think ahead and plan in your mind, you can create a vision. Let it be very particular and not something that is vaguely depicted.

To develop a powerful vision for your life, you need to develop a positive mindset. The only thing standing in your way is TIME. Without positive thinking, there is no vision. Without a vision, there are no goals achieved in life.

Chapter 3
THE POWER OF PLANNING YOUR TIME

Planning your time should be one of the qualities that you take very seriously if you desire to make the most of your life. It is rightly said that a person who does not respect time does not respect his or her own self.

How would one define time management? Is it about making a timetable and abiding by it? Or is it about allotting a specific time to do your daily tasks? Or is it about separating time for work, play, food, and everything else that a human needs to do?

If you put it simply, time management is all about scheduling your tasks in any way that ensures you accomplish what is important to YOU. There should be no wastefulness of time. Even entertainment and recreation— two very important human necessities—should be accounted for. Save enough time for every kind of activity: work, play, and recreation. And most importantly, make time for your family as well. If you only allot time for work, then your time management will backfire because you will be stressed out.

At times we take on additional tasks and we already have so many different things to do throughout the day. However, our time resources are limited. And when we stretch ourselves too thin, we can become burned out. Always prioritize your work. Give priority to things that are more important, those that have an influence on other things that you do. If there is some task whose fulfillment will expedite another task, then do that task first. Proper prioritization can lead to better productivity.

Schedule Planning Time

Time management experts recommend using a personal planning tool to improve your productivity. Examples of personal planning tools include electronic planners, calendars, index cards, and notebooks. Writing down your tasks, schedules, and memory joggers can free your mind to focus on your priorities. The key is to find one planning tool that works for you and use that tool consistently. Schedule a weekly planning appointment for yourself.

A great time for this appointment is on Sundays. I have found this to be the best day to schedule out my business week. If another day works better for you, then by all means, utilize it. This will give you the opportunity to plan for the coming week.

The Three P's of Time

Time is the most valuable commodity. We never seem to have enough of it. Everyone is time-short, time-deprived, time-famished; choose your cliché. Time is what we want most, but what we use worst. Which raises this question: Why don't we value time as we do any other good or service? In order to effectively value your time, you need to first categorize it. These are not types of activities but rather the types of time available to you:

Personal Time: is the time you invest replenishing your mind, body, and soul. The improper use of this time affects your health.

Productive Time: is the time you invest in income-producing activities. The improper use of this time affects your income.

Priority Time: is the time you invest in your family and important relationships. The improper use of this time affects your relationships.

Personal Time

This is the time you spend in replenishment: eating, exercising, sleeping, relaxing, etc. Personal time is the most important time and is necessary to support productive and priority time.

Productive Time

This is the time in which you have to perform whatever it is you do that produces your livelihood. If your business hours are from 9 to 5, that is your productivity time.

Priority Time

This is the time that you invest in things that are important to YOU. Priority time is often invested in the relationships we value most.

Even the busiest people find time for what they want to do and feel is important. Scheduling is not just recording what you have to do (e.g., meetings and appointments), it is also making a time commitment to the things you want to do. Good scheduling requires that you know yourself. Create your Three P's of Time log; you should have determined those times during the day when you are most productive and energized. Schedule time for your personal and high priority activities first, and protect that time from interruptions.

While these three faces of time have definite dividing lines, some overlap and occur sporadically. A business lunch could be productive time and priority time.

Get OUT!

Optimum Use of Time ("OUT") is time spent toward reaching our purpose in the best possible way. This use of time differs for as many purposes and goals people have, so OUT varies for everyone.

So first determine what your OUT is. For example, an outside sales professional's OUT might be spent by being in front of prospects. Another sales professional's OUT may be making sales calls.

Secondly, you must know when your value time is. When is the best time of the day and the best days to reach your OUT?

A sales professional selling to businesses would probably have a prime time between 9 to 5, Monday through Friday. This professional only produces new business when they are face to face with a prospect, so he or she must schedule appointments to be in front of decision makers every hour during prime time.

Obviously with travel, planning, scheduling, checking on product deliveries, and following up with customers, spending every second selling to prospects is not feasible. As a professional, you may be frequently interrupted or pulled in different directions. While you cannot eliminate interruptions, you do get a say on how much time you will spend on them and how much time you will spend on selling to potential clients.

A sales professional could maximize OUT by:

- ✓ Doing as many OUT *support activities* as possible outside of prime time hours, such as entering orders, planning, and scheduling after 5.

- ✓ Scheduling appointments in a desirable geographic sequence.

- ✓ Simultaneously – Placing calls and following up while traveling between appointments.

In order to define your personal OUT, make a list of everything you do that directly helps you reach your goals (personal, productive, and priority time).

Tracking Your Time

Enter how much time each scheduled task takes during your day. This will help you understand how much you can get done during the course of a day and where your precious moments are going. You will see how much time is actually invested producing results and how much time is wasted on unproductive conversations and actions. Be sure to make notes of any interruptions. Label tasks and appointments as OUT or as OUT support activity. Categorize these tasks and assignments by personal, productive, and priority time. At the end of each week, use this information to:

- ✓ Evaluate what percentage of your time is spent in each area of your time
- ✓ See what percentage of your activities is important and what is urgent
- ✓ Discover the ratio between planned and unplanned activities
- ✓ Spot interrupters and time stealers
- ✓ Find out how much time your usual tasks actually take
- ✓ Adjust time estimating for future tasks
- ✓ Make decisions regarding projects, workflow, and delegation

- ✓ Eliminate unneeded tasks
- ✓ Better organize time and tasks

Eliminating Procrastination

Most people procrastinate occasionally, some people procrastinate about almost everything, while others only procrastinate about certain projects or tasks. Some people believe they work better under pressure. This is almost always a fallacy. People applying this pressure to their lives most always perform below their potential. Chronic procrastination can lead to undue stress, and even depression, and often requires behavioral change.

Procrastination

☐ **Get It Done**

☐ **Do It Later**

☐ I'll make a decision at another time.

In order to change habits of procrastination, you must determine why you procrastinate.

There are three major reasons for procrastination:
1. Perfectionism
Many procrastinators tend to be perfectionists. When faced with anything too challenging, they can become paralyzed and shut down.

2. Emotional Avoidance
The emotions associated with a particular chore can be overwhelming. Many people avoid the task to avoid the emotion.

3. Fear
Fear can be paralyzing. Fear of other's reactions, fear of change, fear of risk, and even fear of success can immobilize some people.

Here are some tips on how to stop dragging your feet:
- ✓ Try imagining the task as completed. How do you feel?
- ✓ Talk to the person or people involved. Ask them how your procrastination is affecting them.
- ✓ Try breaking the task down into pieces and doing one part each day.
- ✓ Put the task on your schedule
- ✓ Avoid other procrastinators.

✓ Start a 'no procrastination' program. Set a deadline for every task.

"Vision without action is merely a dream. Action without vision just passes the time. Vision with action can change YOUR world." - **CEO Roundtable**

How to Protect Your Plan

If you spent several hours creating your plan, why would you disrespect yourself and your time by allowing others to destroy it? Protecting your plan is about learning how to respect your own time.

Avoid Interruptions – Do not answer unimportant calls during your productive and priority time blocks in your plan. Learn to screen your calls by having an assistant or through voicemail. Do not allow email pop-ups while working at your computer.

Be Flexible – No matter how well you plan, things happen that you will have no control over: events or occurrences that suddenly take up unplanned time. Build some flexibility into your schedule to allow for unexpected delays, interruptions, and things that take longer than expected. Your appointment might not show or a prospect could be late. Keep other productive activities available as a plan B to substitute at any given time.

Keep Meeting Times and Have an Agenda – Start meetings promptly; this shows that you respect the time of those who are attending the meeting. Follow the agenda. If this is not a meeting that you have scheduled and there is no agenda, simply ask, "Can we take a minute to get clear on the purpose and topics for the meeting to make sure we accomplish what you need?"

Be Prepared – Schedule time between activities to prepare for the next activity. Remember OUT (Optimum Use of Time).

Be Realistic – Be as accurate as possible about the amount of time you allot for activities. Effective planning often depends on your ability to accurately gauge the amount of time required to accomplish a given task, whether that task is to complete an application for new business or to complete a meeting with a client.

Give Yourself Time – While most people are optimistic and start out with great expectations, if you are not used to following a schedule, start slow. Change can be difficult and there are times when it is very challenging to leave our comfort zone and dive into the unknown. When it comes to change, it is very important to understand that you need to give yourself time to evolve.

Make It a Team Effort and Inform Others – Make sure your family, friends, team, clients, and other associates know you are going to be following a new schedule. You might be surprised how many people will help you protect your plan. The best way to do this is to inform those involved that you are on a schedule; tell them how much time you have and explain that your business needs to be concluded within that time restriction. Whether you are at a lunch, in a personal meeting, or on a phone call, politely but firmly let the other person know how much time you have available.

Respect Other People's Time – Showing up late or keeping people waiting is disrespectful. Disrespecting others' time is impudent. Time is the very substance of life. Keeping people waiting for appointments and meetings does not show that you are important, it shows that you are impolite. If you want people to respect your time, start by respecting theirs.

Be Definite About Your Time – Give people specific times when you are available for impromptu meetings or conversations. Some people might be used to 'popping in' throughout your day. Be strict but give them time to adjust to your schedule. (This does not mean you should surrender to any negative time wasters.)

Blame It on the Clock! – When people have reached the end of their appointment or time slot, simply state, "The clock says I have to go now," or "According to the clock, I have to get to my next meeting." This gets you off the hook, and you'll find most people will not object; it's hard to argue with the clock.

After you have determined where your time is going, you can then create goals to rid yourself of your own personal time wasters. Set goals and keep track of whether or not you are accomplishing them. Use organizational tools to help you complete your goals. You may prefer a Day Planner, a software program such as Microsoft Outlook, or an iPhone. Whatever tool you choose to use, prioritize each day's tasks. Determine what tasks must be done today and what tasks need to be accomplished in the future. The goal is to "Get It Done."

Chapter 4
THE POWER OF MANAGING YOUR PRIORITIES

There are specific skills and steps that you can learn to effectively manage multiple priorities—and to actually assess which activities you need to work on first—to get things done on your daily and weekly schedule. We all know the feeling of getting up for work in the morning having so much to do that we do not know where to start. Oftentimes, everything that we have on our list seems like a priority, which makes it tough to figure out where to begin.

The ability to choose and complete projects in the order of importance is more challenging for some than for others. When something is really important, it's easy to get caught up in the details and end up spending way too much time on a project. Spending too much time on one priority, however, prevents you from getting other things done on your "Get It Done" list. Acknowledge when you are doing this and enforce strict deadlines to prevent yourself from getting stuck on one project for too long.

In order to choose a project in its order of importance, you must be aware of how many projects you have for the day or week and the timeline in which they must be completed. In order to do this, every planning session you schedule you must create a "Get It Done" list.

List all your projects; write down everything that needs to get done that for that day or week. Once you have created your list, rate them as "important" versus "unimportant" to determine the top priorities for that day. When all tasks and projects are rated, use these additional filters to prioritize:

- ✓ Imagine the consequences of eliminating the task. This exercise will often remove some unneeded tasks altogether.
- ✓ Decide if each task should be performed in productive time or priority time.
- ✓ Determine who will be affected by the project if it's not completed.

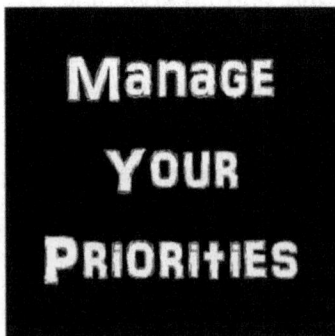

Manage Your Priorities

IMPORtant

_____
_____

UnIMPORtant

_____
_____

Does This Task or Project Make Sense? Does every task contribute to your big picture? If you want to start living a life that has meaning, then choose a clear direction for yourself. When you have the courage to say, "This is important to me and I'm going after it," you do not fall into the trap of taking on unnecessary projects. While not always possible, everything you do should contribute to your objectives.

The Measures of a Project Value

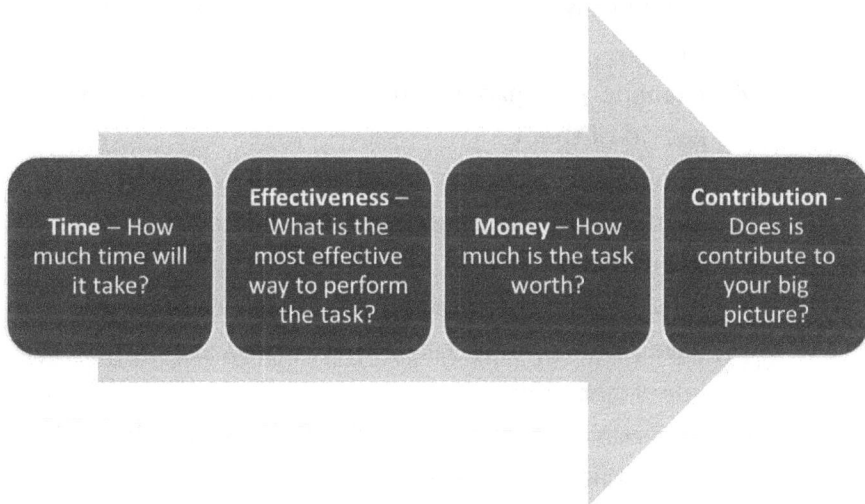

Time – How much time will it take?	Effectiveness – What is the most effective way to perform the task?	Money – How much is the task worth?	Contribution - Does is contribute to your big picture?

Behavioral Changes for Effective Time Management

✓ Clarify your goals. Revise them weekly. Keep a list in a place where you will see them daily.

- ✓ Do not rely on your memory only. Keep information in a trusted system where you can organize and classify it.
- ✓ Plan your week at the beginning of each week. Sundays are a great day to plan. You should have a clear "Get It Done" list for every workday.
- ✓ Set completion dates.
- ✓ Create a system to notify yourself of scheduled tasks.
- ✓ Prioritize and focus.
- ✓ Continually evaluate your progress at the end of the day.
- ✓ Examine your habits. If they are harmful or useless, get rid of them.
- ✓ Avoid procrastination by scheduling every task. If anything must be postponed, reschedule immediately.
- ✓ Reward yourself when you get things done as you have planned, especially if these things are important to you.
- ✓ Be flexible. Always have a Plan B. If you are delayed or waiting for something or somebody, make use of this time.
- ✓ Delegate tasks whenever possible.
- ✓ Ask for help when you need it.
- ✓ Keep negative people out of your environment.
- ✓ Enjoy the process. Be optimistic and positive about your life.

How much of your work day is actually productive? Think about how you are interrupted during your OUT (Optimum Use of Time). Most of us spend countless hours on repeating tasks we have already done, reacting to situations that should never have arisen, and ranting about how much we have to do and what little time we have to do them. Have you ever kept track of how many times you are interrupted or distracted throughout the day. Make a list of every kind of interruption you have experienced in the last week:

Tracking Interruptions

Interruption	People	Process	Device	Time Lost
Totals				

STOP: Did you complete the exercises? Are you just reading to say you know or are you working for full understanding? I desire the best for you, so if you have not done the exercise and you refuse to participate, put this book down; it is not for the fainthearted. I want results in your life, so please complete all exercises.

I know this exercise can be extremely tedious and seem to take up even more of your precious time but in order to improve time management, we have to become aware of where our time goes. As the Roman philosopher Seneca said, "You tend to use time as if you had more and more forever."

After you have completed your log, analyze it. Look for time stealers. A time stealer is anything that reduces your effectiveness in the workplace. Examples include: doing work that you should have delegated, spending too much time answering or sending emails, unnecessary telephone conversations, interruptions by other employees, long-winded meetings, rushing through projects that should have been completed at an earlier date, trying to accomplish too many things at once, redoing other people's work because it is not up to par, doing tasks more than once, lack of skills or knowledge, poor planning, lack of sleep, inability to say "no," and lack of a plan for your day. Where does your time go?

"The individual who masters himself or herself through self-discipline can never be mastered by others." **Dr. Dennis Kimbro**

The purpose of life is to enjoy it and live it to the fullest. Life is too short to waste doing anything you do not enjoy. Earl Nightingale stated in his bestselling audio program *The Strangest Secret*, "Your returns in life are exactly what you gave." There is a huge difference between living a positive, productive life and barely existing or surviving. How and why we live is much more important than simply living. It should come as no surprise that more often than not, the people who end up being successful in life are the ones who know exactly what they want and they take the time to write their goals and focus on their desires while taking action daily to achieve their goals.

Chapter 5
THE POWER OF BEING ORGANIZED

Are you working too hard because you just cannot seem to get organized? Organizational skills are perhaps the most undervalued trait of successful business men and women. Although I consider myself an organized person, my life has not always been this way. My life was unorganized until I begin to work in corporate America. In a corporate environment, productivity is expected and highly valued. The foundation for productivity is organization skills and my foundation was very unstable.

There were times when senior management would come to my office and ask me for very important reports and those reports would be under a pile of papers with coffee stains on them. Don't judge me. If you have ever had to search through endless stacks of business papers to find the one document that you need, you know the value of being organized.

I used to whine about being too busy to develop the necessary organizational skills, even though I knew it would help me be more productive. The truth is, it was the fear of failure, peer pressure, and discomfort at the thought of leaving my normal routine that lulled me to settle instead of going for what I truly wanted.

It was because of the corporate executive mentoring program I joined that I realized if I wanted to advance, I needed to become extremely organized. So this became a strong incentive for me to refine my organizational skills. Most organized people aren't keeping everything in order just for their own amusement—they're doing it for a reason. Although there were other factors, I believe being highly organized helped me to rise rapidly through the corporate ranks.

"Organizing is what you do before you do something, so that when you do it, it is not all mixed up." - **A.A. Milne**

The value of organizational skills becomes even more crucial when you are an entrepreneur. When my partners and I began building our consultant business, we found that we all needed to strengthen our organizational skills. We could not afford to waste our energy on things that did not lead to income-producing activities. We all had families to provide for. I know I couldn't go home at the end of the day and tell my family I was answering emails all day. They wanted to know if I was doing what was necessary to put food on the table. Unlike college or the corporate world, when you are an entrepreneur, everything rests on your shoulders. One of the keys to making the entrepreneurial lifestyle easier, less stressful, and fun is being highly organized.

Having good organizational skills is about making the best use of your time. Being organized reduces the amount of time you have to dig to uncover important business information. When you are the leader of an organization, you need to know where your time goes. For example, if you are responding to emails every ten minutes, you might want to create an autoresponder to more effectively handle your inbox.

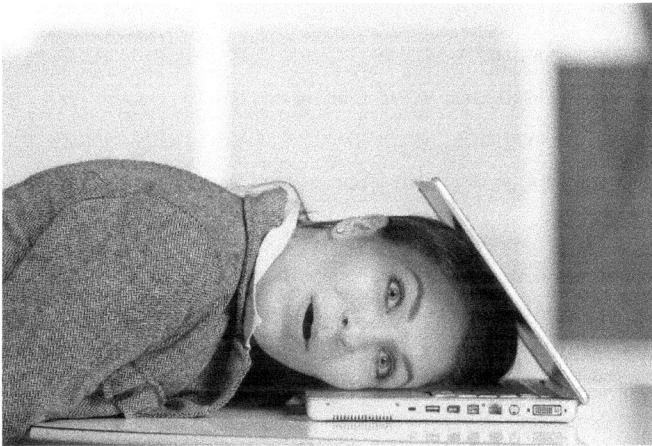

An autoresponder is a program that automatically generates a set response to all messages sent to a particular e-mail address. You control your life. Whatever electronics you use, make them work for YOU, not the other way around. Do you really have to keep checking your email every ten minutes? Maybe, but I bet you will be more productive if you set up an autoresponder and then respond to emails at a scheduled time. After all, there are so many tools and one to fit everyone, so use what works but make it work for you!

Reasons for Being Organized:
- ✓ Become more productive
- ✓ Saves you the most important resource…TIME
- ✓ Saves you energy
- ✓ Can possibly save you money
- ✓ Become focused and purposeful
- ✓ Increases the probability of promotions at work
- ✓ Reduces stress
- ✓ Increases your confidence
- ✓ Provides an example for your organization
- ✓ Helps you be more efficient and effective

Unapologetically take control of your time and priorities. Keep analyzing where you are spending your time on a weekly basis and make adjustments to what you should be doing and how you are doing it. We all get off track from time to time so don't beat yourself up about it, just take stock and move forward.

How many dreams and goals have you evaded because you were afraid of failing? How many times have you looked back on your life, looked upon the mistakes that you have made, and beat yourself up over them? So many people allow the dread of making mistakes to hold them back!

If you fail at something, it touches you in a deep emotional way. While it feels detrimental at the time, it teaches you imperative lessons. You learn what does not work and that which might truly bring you closer to success. Because it is so disturbing to fail, if you have the courage to get back up and try again, you will try harder the next time.

Even if you try and fail, you will never be the same person you were before you started the project. "*The father of success is work - the mother of achievement is ambition.*" You have forced yourself to a new level, moved away from your comfort zone, and are much more sensible for having tried the task. If you constantly avoid pursuing goals and ambitions because you are scared of making mistakes, you will never realize what you can accomplish. Trying and failing is better than never trying at all.

Success is not measured by the position that you have achieved but by the obstacles which you had to overcome. After experiencing failure, you might feel hurt, broken, and/or disappointed.

However, something astonishing happens once the original sting wears thin: you truly become stronger in mind and spirit! With each effort you put forth, you grow stronger in character and better your odds of achieving success. Success consists of getting up just one more time after you have failed.

If you put your efforts into trying something and you fall short, you build bravery to try again. It is the fear of the unknown that truly holds people back; however, when you have taken the risk and lost, it won't feel as chilling the next time you try. Courage doesn't come from winning but from the quest of goals, whether you win or not.

You don't have to lie awake at night to succeed; just stay awake during the day and be willing to do what's necessary.

Chapter 6
THE POWER OF GOOD DECISION MAKING

Many people waste an enormous amount of time because they just cannot make up their mind. Agonizing over decisions can interrupt all Three Faces of Time. Sleepless nights can violate personal time, which can leave you depleted and less productive. Making sound decisions is a skill set that needs to be developed like any other. Few people have analyzed their own decision making process. As a consultant who works with many entrepreneurs on a consistent basis, I can tell you with great certainty all leaders are not created equal when it comes to the competency of their decision making skills. Nothing will test your leadership mettle more than your ability to make decisions.

What should I do?
Which way should I go?

Until a decision is made and acted upon, nothing happens. No one can decide for you. If you want to control the direction of your life, you must develop the habit of making good decisions. Making wise decisions is one of life's greatest challenges. Show me someone who has not made a bad decision and I will show you someone who is a little short on telling the truth, or someone who avoids making decisions at all costs. *"The purpose of a decision is not to find the perfect option. The purpose of a decision is to get you to the next decision."* – **CEO Roundtable**

It is not what you do once in a while that has an impact on the direction of your life, it is what you do consistently. Decide today that you are not going to live in mediocrity.

"In any moment of decision, the best thing you can do is the right thing, the next best thing is the wrong thing, and the worst thing you can do is nothing." - **Theodore Roosevelt**

Life is made up of little and big decisions and how a man or woman decides determines the course of his or her life. Successful people know how to make decisions. If you do not learn how to make good decisions, you will continue to have the kind of results you had up until now. Deciding creates the purpose; it gives you a goal—a reason to do what you do. Once a decision is made, carrying it out becomes a matter of will, courage, and dedication.

Make a decision today to develop yourself to the point where you can achieve your personal goals and gain mastery over managing your activities. Decide who you want to become. Describe exactly what you will look like when you become successful in your personal and professional life. Your decision to live a balanced life is not an overnight success. There is some work that is required.

Making a decision can be exciting and stressful so to help you deal with these emotions objectively; you need to use a structured approach. We are going to evaluate some decision-making techniques and strategies you can use to become a better decision maker. Some choices are simple and seem straight forward, while others are complex and require a multi-step approach to making the decision.

Decision Making Techniques

Consequence Technique: Does your decision align with who you are as a person? Have you thought about the repercussions of not making a decision? Does this decision go against your beliefs? Making a decision that goes against your personal beliefs may bring you short term gain but in the long run, you always have to live with the decisions that you made. Imagine the consequences of your decisions, good and bad.

Fantasizing Technique: Many times, we limit ourselves to our present position when making decisions. While this is practical, a simple fantasizing technique can open your mind to new ideas. In order to open your mind to possibilities, try fantasizing about your position. For example, what is the perfect outcome for your decision? By reframing the way, we look at our decisions, we can gain new perspectives about the choices we have to make.

Mentor Technique: When you are up against the wall and cannot make a definite decision, having mentors you can run things by can make all the difference. Make sure you consult with someone you trust and most importantly, seek a mentor who is not going to give you biased information. These mentors do not need to be in your industry but they must have a history of making good decisions. What I have found, and my mentor expressed this to me a million times, is that success leaves clues.

In Their Shoes Technique: Try to imagine the perspective of everyone else involved in the decision and/or affected by the decision. If needed, ask people involved how they believe different decisions will affect them. They will have insights and information that will affect the choices you make, and this will help you make better decisions. Furthermore, it pays for you to gain their buy-in as you often have to rely on them to implement your decisions.

Inductive Reasoning: See the big picture and imagine the different outcomes of your decisions. Draw conclusions based on your past experience in similar situations and the experiences of others. Base your hypothesis on as many facts as possible.

Cost-Benefit Analysis: Weigh the costs of alternative decisions and estimate the benefits. Many of us are guilty of rushing decisions, particularly when there is a deadline looming and we are under pressure. But rather than making a snap decision, make sure you consider the cost-benefit analysis. While all other applicable techniques should be exhausted, this one should be one of the first used.

The Art of Stopping: In order to avoid jumping to the wrong conclusions or in order to gather facts, stop and ask: "When does this decision need to be made?" Consider the consequences of holding off on making a decision. This will give you the time to collect more data and verify information.

Decision Value: Estimate the cost to make a decision. Often, the costs of studies made to reach decisions have been costly than the outcome of the choice that was made. Weigh the time and manpower that will be needed to make the decision. Know the value of making a decision.

Pros and Cons: This is one of the oldest but still reliable decision-making strategies. Draw two columns and list the benefits of a decision on one side and the disadvantages on the other. Weigh the results. By making your plans and decisions based on the most likely pros/cons scenarios, you can be confident that they are sound, even if circumstances change.

In order to gain control over your life, you must take your power back and learn how to allow yourself to be what you have envisioned. You are responsible for ruling your own actions and decisions. To make consistently good decisions, take the right action when needed and refrain from the wrong action, which requires character and self-discipline.

Good Decision
Making Skills

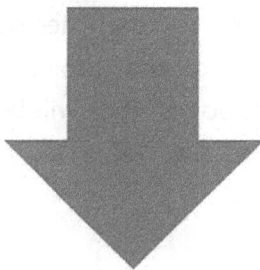

Bad Decision
Making Skills

Chapter 7
THE POWER OF EFFECTIVE COMMUNICATION

A recent study suggested that the number one time waster in business today is from communication confusion. Effective communication is one of the most important life skills we can learn yet one we do not usually put a lot of effort into. There are seven important points which can give you the skills to communicating effectively.

1. Completeness will bring the desired response: Completeness means that whatever you communicate should be complete and there should be no missing facts in your speech. Oftentimes, people assume that some facts are known by the audience or listeners. This is not the right approach because if you started to assume, you would not be able to give all the details of the core objective. The whole idea will become confused and you will be facing trouble in making others understand. You should provide detailed information to your listeners and in fact, you should provide some additional information to make your points clearer.

While preparing your presentation or report, you should make sure that you are answering all possible questions which your topic can have. In this way, your audience will be more responsive about your topic and they will ask you more logical questions. It often happens that after you finish your presentation, someone may ask: "What are you actually trying to say?"

This is probably the worst comment that you can get after a presentation, but it should make you wonder why that person was confused by what you said. To avoid such embarrassing situations, you should make sure your presentation is thoroughly researched and complete without ignoring any facts. Completeness brings the desired response from your audience. You need to include everything that you think is related to your topic of discussion and try to describe both positive and negative approaches.

"Wise men speak because they have something to say; Fools because they have to say something." - **Plato**

2. Conciseness will save time: Conciseness is another important aspect of effective communication, especially when you talk about business communication. Your message should be concise because this will make it more proper and to the point. Time is important in modern day life and no one has the time to listen to a full hour presentation while you can deliver the same presentation in 30 minutes. Besides, if you add an unnecessary pause, repeat information, and use other similar tactics to prolong the duration, then your audience will get bored and they will prefer to either leave the discussion or they will stop taking interest. You should only include relevant facts about your topic and avoid using unnecessary information.

For example, if you are making a presentation about the annual budget for your organization, then you should keep facts to the point and avoid giving irrelevant examples for cutting down the budget or increasing it. Your aim is to present the report of your annual budget and this does not mean that you should add suggestions because that may be designated to someone else. So, make your information concise and save time for yourself as well as for your audience.

Communication Blunders:
*   Giving Poor Instructions
*   Inability to Listen to Instructions
*   Causing Personal/Emotional Discord
*   Miscommunication of Ideas
*   Irrelevant Communication
*   Counter Productive Communication
*   Confusing Communication/Mixed Messages
*   Inappropriate Communication
*   Dishonesty

"The single biggest problem in communication is the illusion that it has taken place." - **George Bernard Shaw**

3. Consideration means understanding of human nature: Consideration is one of the most important things in effective communication because it will make sure that you understand the receiver in a better way. This means that you have to think twice about saying certain things and make sure that you are always conveying your message in a positive tone.

If there are some negative points in your discussion, then you should overcome those by emphasizing the positive points. In proper and effective consideration, it is important to understand that the more you explain benefits to your audience, the more interesting your discussion will become. So you should explain each and every benefit of your discussion which will make people more attentive and they will be more interested in integrating those benefits into their lives.

Focus more on "you" instead of 'I" or "We." This also sends a pleasant impression that you actually care more about others instead of yourself. There is a saying that states, "Think before you speak," and this most likely refers to being considerate.

"Take advantage of every opportunity to practice your communication skills so that when important occasions arise, you will have the gift, the style, the sharpness, the clarity, and the emotions to affect other people." – **Jim Rohn**

You should properly analyze everything before presenting it to others. Analyze everything from the receiver's point of view because that will allow you to think about those questions which are often neglected by following just one approach. You should avoid the use of negative expressions like, "I hate." Instead, replace them with "I prefer." How we use our words have tremendous power. Words give out energy and a message which creates a reaction in others. Everything you say produces an effect in the world. Whatever you say to someone else will produce some kind of an effect in that person. We are constantly creating something, either positive or negative with our words.

4. Concreteness reinforces confidence: Concreteness means that you should be specific and accurate about the facts and figures which you represent in your discussion. The facts should be clear, and being accurate is even more important because people often give value to words and especially figures which you represent. Verb choice should also be vivid and wording should be such that it should create a positive image of your overall topic. If you start to sound a little vague, obscure, and general about your facts, then things will start to get confusing. Emphasis on one topic will be lost and as a result, the effectiveness of communication will not be present.

If you are presenting some solid and true facts and figures, then it will automatically boost your confidence. You should try to gather figures from different surveys, and the Internet can be a good place to do this research, no matter what kind of topic you have. You can share your opinion then see how your audience responds. But you should remember that all facts and figures should be specific and related to your core topic and they should not be irrelevant.

5. Clarity can make communication more comprehensive: Clarity is often mistaken by people and they think that making the fact more clear is clarity, but clarity is more about making your speech and exact message better. You need to choose your words precisely and use simpler language to convey your message. The simpler your language, the easier it will be for the audience to decode your message and get hold of your idea clearly. Best way to bring clarity is to use simpler words and create easy to understand paragraphs. Do not be too formal with the choice of words and remain casual in your approach.

If you try to be too formal in your approach and use heavy language, then it is a known fact that not everyone will be able to understand that complex language.

As it is mentioned in the heading, clarity makes your message more comprehensive, so make your message as clear as possible and try to use fewer and simpler words in it so that everyone can understand it.

6. Courtesy makes relations stronger: Courtesy means that you show respect to the receiver. When it comes to business communication, your message should start with a respectful word and end with a respectful clause as well. This is just a way of giving value to the feeling of the receiver. Always think about the caliber of the audience. Use nondiscriminatory expressions because that will convince the other person that you value their thoughts. If you are being appreciative, thoughtful, respectful, and using polite words and gestures, then the receiver will feel good about your discussion and will start to take interest even more.

You can take an example that if an email comes to you starting with a simple "Hi" or "Hello," then you may not value it. But if the same email comes with stating, "Hello our respectful and valued customer," then you will value the message more. Use of polite language shows a form of professionalism.

7. Correctness will avoid all the confusion:
You should know the social, educational, and religious background of the reader or audience and then use your

language according to that background. All of these features will make your communication more effective.

If you start to make your language ambiguous and improper or you have too many punctuation and grammar mistakes, then people will not value your message; and in the end, it will be regarded as ineffective communication. But you can change this easily by adding some true facts and figures and keeping your grammar simple and correct.

Now these are the 7 Cs of communication and if you can learn to control all of them, then you will have an effective communication method. In short, you know that when your message is concise, complete, considerate, correct, clear, courteous, and concrete, it will be an effective message.

Chapter 8
THE POWER OF DELEGATING

There is nothing more exciting than breaking free of sitting behind a desk doing tedious work that someone else can do much better. The power of delegating is a skill that can be learned. Delegation involves giving someone else the responsibility and authority to do something you normally do and holding them accountable for doing it. Many people suffer from: "If I don't it, it won't get done right."

At our annual seminar, Emerging Business Boot Camp, we surveyed all the business leaders in attendance and asked why they choose not to delegate: 25% of them said they do not delegate because they "have trust issues with other people doing the job."

Know what you are worth... It can save you time!

My mentor once said: "If you could do the activities that have the biggest impact on your business in terms of profit and expansion and just focus on that all day, every day, what would the impact be on your business?"

These were wise words! This is where the power of delegation comes in. By outsourcing everyday tasks and building a network of reliable partners, you can free yourself to focus on more important business matters; for example, bringing the best clients to your business.

Many entrepreneurs think that by "letting go" of certain tasks or hiring someone else to do them, it takes away from their bottom line: profits. There may be financial decisions you have to make before you decide if the idea of delegating is right for you. Make sure that you consider the pros and cons but if you need to do it, there is no reason to wait! You will be able to get more done! The effective delegating of tasks is an indispensable skill for entrepreneurs, leaders, managers, and heads of households, and it is a direct contributor to good time management.

DELEGATE

Entrepreneurs and leaders are usually 'take charge' people. They know their businesses better than anyone and can perform most jobs within their organization. These leaders often refuse to let go of tasks which can easily be delegated to someone else. You must be the visionary and driver on the important issues in regards to building your organization, but the question you need to ask yourself is: "Do people see me as a control freak?"

As a leader, you must decide which jobs would be better off delegated or outsourced. Let go of any duty which would be better delegated. Focus on the things that matter most to you. Let others who are capable focus on the customer service or fulfillment of orders. Let someone with technical skills handle the technical issues. When you focus on what matters most to you, you'll be able to get more done.

> Some people might do the job differently than you but effectively reach the same results.

Question every task in front of you. Decide who, beside yourself, could perform each one. If this is difficult, imagine if you were somehow restricted to only delegating. Who would do your job? When possible, give those on your team choices. Ask them to decide what tasks they would like to assume. Remember, delegating should give you more of the precious resource called time. There is a fine line between successful delegating and failure from others' incompetence. Save time and money by hiring the experts. Someone who has vast experience will be able to work more quickly and efficiently than you, especially if you're unfamiliar with the task. It's okay to let the experts handle it.

When should you outsource? Bringing in experts can be expensive. The real question here is: "Am I losing business because I am consistently doing non-income-producing activities?"

✓ Are you prioritizing your time well?
✓ If yes, are you struggling to grow your business?
✓ Will hiring an expert increase your cash flow?

If taking care of the day to day operations is preventing you from focusing on income-producing activities, you need to hire help. No task should get in the way of actual income-producing activities.

Delegated Tasks Checklist

- ✓ Put your plan in writing and document progress.
- ✓ Clarify your goal. Make sure the person or people understand the desired results.
- ✓ Create a visual picture of the expected outcome.
- ✓ Determine criteria to analyze results.
- ✓ Make results measurable.
- ✓ Determine challenges delegates might encounter, such as budget restraints, time conflicts, etc.
- ✓ Keep directions as simple as possible.
- ✓ Review the action plan regularly. If you have any new information, make changes in your plan and share with the team.
- ✓ Monitor delegated activity. Set task milestones and have people report results to you at critical intervals.

Whenever possible, have a Plan B for delegated tasks that fall short of completion or produce undesirable results.

Outsourcing

Many entrepreneurs have discovered the benefits of outsourcing, from projects to accounting services. The time to locate vendors, check references, evaluate services, collect bids, and make payment plans must be weighed for each service or project. To get your feet wet, try posting a simple job on an online outsourcing service.

Outsourcing Tips

- ✓ Don't commit to long-term contracts.
- ✓ Make sure you have a clear contract.
- ✓ Communicate effectively.
- ✓ Define your project clearly.
- ✓ Be firm about deadlines.
- ✓ Be flexible about ideas from vendors.
- ✓ Be sure you understand the terms and charges.
- ✓ Pay all vendors as promised.

Delegation is one of the most crucial productivity skills in effective time management. If you are having trust issues in regards to delegating, face your fears. When you leverage the skills and talents of your team members and hired outsourced experts, you can save your time and start focusing on those things that matter most to you. No one said you had to do it all alone.

"As all entrepreneurs know, you live and die by your ability to prioritize. You must focus on the most important, mission-critical tasks each day and night, and then share, delegate, delay or skip the rest." - **CEO Roundtable**

Chapter 9
THE POWER OF TIME SAVING TOOLS

There are many types of tools that will save you time and increase your productivity if you utilize them. In this chapter, my only hope is that you apply some of the time saving strategies so that you can spend more time on what really matters in your life—BEING PRODUCTIVE.

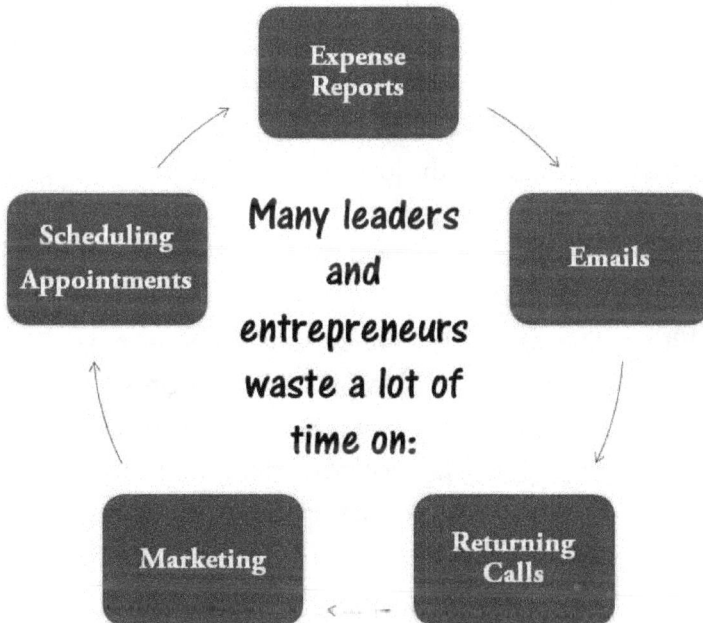

Expense Reports

Scheduling Appointments

Many leaders and entrepreneurs waste a lot of time on:

Emails

Marketing

Returning Calls

The items listed above are only a few of the many time wasters that can affect your productivity. This is why I advocate for finding areas in your life and business that you can automate.

"The first rule of any technology used in a business is that automation applied to an efficient operation will magnify the efficiency. The second is that automation applied to an inefficient operation will magnify the inefficiency." - **Bill Gates**

So let's explore different ways you can automate certain areas of your life/business. I have created a list of online tools you can use to save time:

Online Calendar

Scheduling meetings with clients is one of the most difficult and intricate responsibilities of a business. I was frustrated after I discovered how much time I would spend emailing clients back and forth, just to figure out a time to meet that fit both of our schedules. One day I would like to thank the inventors of the online calendar. This tool has saved me so much time and relieved me of my frustration. With online calendars, you schedule meetings by checking your partner or clients availability in a single view. You can create a calendar that's accessible to everyone in your organization. This is a very powerful time saving tool. This works when you want to set appointments, arrange group meetings, and schedule interviews. You can put in your availability and then those who want to set times for meetings can quickly see what's available. No more back and forth emails for me. **Caution:** You don't want to share your calendar with someone who has a habit of stealing your time.

All sorts of technology products promise to reduce manual tasks in your business, but online calendars really can help. Online calendars are a reliable and efficient method to schedule appointments. The more you promote it to the people within your organization and with your clients, the more they will use it. As a result, you will spend less time sending emails and making calls just to schedule appointments. Getting started with a professional online scheduling system can be free and easy to setup.

Backup Systems

Have you ever lost all your data and spent hours trying to recover it? had a hard drive failure? or experienced a bad installation of a software program?

If you are looking to avoid wasting your time on technical issues, you have to implement a system to backup all the data files on your computer and your business network "just in case" something goes wrong. If you want to maintain productivity, you must keep disaster plans in place and practice prevention. With the availability of backup software and the low cost of external hard drives, there is no excuse for not having daily backups for your computers. One computer crash without a backup can cost you more than just the time to recover; it can ruin your business.

Scanning Documents

With all the time lost looking for paperwork, replacing lost documents, and the space required, every business should invest the time in scanning documents. While this seems like an elementary concept, few businesses fully utilize digital storage. This is one time saver that does require an initial investment of time to scan the documents. But studies have shown that the time required to file, protect, and retrieve documents is a major cost to entrepreneurs.

Email Marketing

What is the best tool to use to stay in contact with your clients? Email marketing. My favorite email marketing tool is Mail Chimp, but there are others you can use as well: Constant Contact, iContact, Vertical Response, or Campaign Monitor. It's all about what tool you feel comfortable using. Email marketing is one of the most effective ways to keep in touch with clients. It's cost effective and if done properly, can help build brand awareness and loyalty. Within our company, we send out monthly newsletters to our clients. By using email marketing, we can have our marketing specialist set up the email campaign to go out at a scheduled time.

By implementing email marketing within your business, you are saving time and keeping your company name in front of important clients. And the great thing about using this tool is that you don't have to be a professional graphic designer. Many of the email marketing tools come with templates ready for use; all you have to do is add the content.

Social Media

Do you know that updating your status every five minutes on social media is not income-producing activity? How can you possibly manage all of your social media platforms? And how do you know who to engage and respond to on social media? You can optimize your social media efforts and responsibilities using some of the many scheduling and automation tools available today. These tools can help fill your queue, quickly sort out and participate in active discussions, as well as simplify a way for others to share your post.

A great social media management tool is Hootsuite. With Hootsuite, you can manage your posts efficiently. You can organize all your social accounts into one dashboard and streamline your workflow. You can select which "streams" you view, which can even include any keywords that you would like to track. You can then schedule multiple posts on multiple platforms simultaneously. You can use services like Hootsuite or Buffer to schedule your posts on Facebook, Twitter, Instagram, and many more to be posted without your assistance. Simply add a post in the queue and it will automatically post when you schedule it, leaving you free to focus on other tasks that really need your attention.

RSS Feeds

How are you getting your news? For many years, news was either read from a newspaper or seen on a television. There was little choice as to what news was reported or when. Now with the advent of the Internet, there is much more news and this news is coming at a faster rate. But what news really benefits you?

Choose Your News: News can be a major distraction. The majority of news is negative because that is what sells. Our life manifests from our most dominant thoughts and feelings. Just as whatever we plant grows, that which we focus our attention on multiplies. You are the fruit of the thoughts you have planted and nourished. If you want a better harvest, you must plant better thoughts. Whatever we put in our minds comes out in our lives. We select the circumstances that occur in our lives by choosing how and where we focus our attention. Every negative thought has a consequence. What news do you really need to be productive in your business? Choose that news by RSS feed. Filter out everything else. Protect your mind at all cost.

Expense Reports

Most people were never trained at managing money. The best way to manage money is by creating a solid budget. If you are running a home-based business or brick and mortar, then more than likely, you oversee a budget. There is no need to be frustrated with creating budgets and expense reports. There are several online tools that can help you. Here are the best online software apps for creating expense reports or organizing receipts:

Shoeboxed

Shoeboxed offers a few different methods for entering receipts into this online software. Shoeboxed is great for managing and storing receipts for expense reports, or tax or insurance documentation.

- ✓ Scan receipts or take a snapshot with a digital camera and send them electronically to Shoeboxed.
- ✓ Forward email receipts you get with online purchases to your Shoeboxed account.
- ✓ Use the iPhone app to scan and submit receipts.
- ✓ Go the old-fashioned snail mail route and mail them in to let Shoeboxed do the scanning and data entry for you.

Expensify

Expensify makes capturing receipts, tracking time or mileage, handling business travel, and creating expense reports quick and easy. Acknowledged by the tech community as the best app for expense reporting,

Expensify takes the time, paper, and headaches out of your expense reports! Simply put, Expensify produces expense reports that are easy to understand. Expensify imports expenses and receipts automatically when you use a credit card or uses your mobile phone to scan receipts (iPhone or Android), submits expense reports via email, and can give you online reimbursements with QuickBooks and direct deposit.

Here's what Expensify does for you:
- ✓ Easy Report Submission: Email expense reports to your office manager or convert to PDF and save
- ✓ Easy Receipt Capture: Simply take a picture of your receipt and then throw it away
- ✓ Mobile Expense Creation: Create and edit expenses on the go—in your car, at the airport, anywhere
- ✓ Mileage Entry: Enter distance using your phone's GPS or take a picture of your odometer
- ✓ Bank and Credit Card Import: Sync your card with Expensify and it will automatically pull your transactions into your account

Make sure you choose the right software that works for you and your organization.

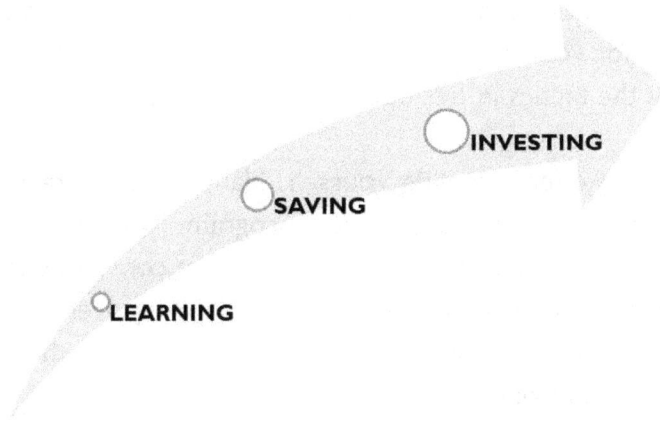

○INVESTING

○SAVING

○LEARNING

Conclusion

The information and strategies in this book can change your bottom line and your life!

Before we can begin to create a vision for what it is we want to do in life, we must first believe we are capable of achieving whatever it is we desire. Without this belief, we would never even attempt to do anything about our dreams. As Otis Redding sang, "We'll be sitting on the dock of the bay, watching the tides roll away...wasting time."

Start everyday with an accomplishment that energizes you. For some, this is a physical workout; for others, prayer. When you start implementing the strategies in effective time management, you will feel in control and have more time for yourself to do the things that matter most to you. Use the tactics in this book to avoid procrastinating.

Do not over schedule yourself. Many people attack time management like any other program, with full steam. Scheduling too much in a day will lead to constant changes, delayed projects, and will leave you feeling overwhelmed. Start slow and build. It's not how you start, it's how you finish. Be flexible.

While any change can feel uncomfortable at first, the rewards of managing your activities effectively are dimensional. You will become more energetic, more productive, more relaxed, and experience greater confidence.

Make it a point to set an example by applying the strategies in effective time management. Tell others within your organization about the strategies you are implementing. If everyone throughout your company along with your clients decides to effectively manage their time, everyone will benefit.

In a world where uncertainty reigns, contemplating the future with a focused plan has a calming effect. Taking control of your time will give you an 'in-charge' feeling and confidence that others will notice.

Remember that saving time requires an investment of time: the time to plan, make changes, and better manage your daily activities.

In life, people are going to tell you that you cannot achieve the dreams you have set out to accomplish. They will tell you that you do not have the ability, potential, skill, or drive. This is the "crabs in the barrel" mentality. Those people who say you cannot achieve your dreams have to keep you down because your success will eliminate their excuses for not being successful. If you listen to them, you will not succeed; you will fail. Do not listen to the cynics and dream killers. Do not listen to those who do not believe in you.

Listen to what God says about you and tell yourself that you will succeed and you will achieve what you set out to do. It takes preparation, knowledge, persistence, and work, but you can do anything you aim to do if you believe in yourself. Be your own #1 fan!

We sincerely hope you found the value in *The Power of Effective Time Management* strategies shared in this book.

The possibilities for your life are endless!

Hasheem Francis is the Co-Founder and CEO of Built To Prosper Companies. With two decades of entrepreneurial and leadership experience, Hasheem Francis is a leadership consultant and advisor to CEOs, business leaders, corporate executives and community leaders across the country. His vast expertise in dealing with business change, along with his strong financial investment background and leadership development skills, enables him to provide unique and unparalleled counsel to a diverse range of industry professionals.
www.BTPCompanies.com

Deborah Francis is the Co-Founder and COO of Built To Prosper Companies. Deborah is an entrepreneur, best-selling author, investor, keynote speaker, recognized industry thought leader, and an expert on business development. Deborah Francis has developed curriculum and delivered training sessions specifically related to entrepreneurship, small business development, and professional development. Deborah has trained, led and mentored hundreds of people with her functional knowledge and educational background. Deborah has a M.A.Ed. Masters in Secondary Education of English.
www.BTPCompanies.com

BUILT TO PROSPER
COMPANIES
Success is Created By Visionaries & Built By Leaders

Built To Prosper Companies
Hasheem Francis & *Deborah Francis*
Co Founder, CEO   Co Founder, COO
Consulting ▪Investing▪ Training

Built To Prosper Companies is an innovative business network that provides strategic investments in a diverse portfolio of companies. As a leading provider of business consulting and training since 1999, Built To Prosper Companies has worked with over 1500 small to mid-sized businesses.

Built To Prosper Companies, specializes in business: planning, marketing, leadership development and raising business investment capital.

Built To Prosper Companies is in business to produce value and unparalleled results for companies by delivering business solutions that support them in driving revenue growth. This is done with an uncompromising commitment toward serving our clients with the utmost in respect, integrity, and the highest standards of excellence. Our delivery model is predicated on exacting alignment with the unique aspects of each client's business strategy, organizational structure, and culture, ensuring each client engagement provides clear and actionable tactics that will drive success on an ongoing, quantifiable basis. We believe that by delivering on this promise, we will help our clients not only drive incremental revenue growth, but also bring more meaning and fulfillment to our clients, their business, and the clients they serve. Built To Prosper Companies is headquartered in Orlando, FL, with affiliate operations in New York, NY, and Hilton Head, SC.

For more information on how we can help your business, visit: www.BTPCompanies.com.

Would You Like to Hire Professional Speakers for Your Next Event? We have a team of experts who specialize in taking care of all our events and making sure we fully understand your needs as an organization. We have been producing amazing results for our clients and seminar participants for over a decade.

Our mission is to empower you and your team with the same tools and strategies that have been used to help millions of people from around the world take their lives to the next level. You and your team are on your way to learning some life-changing skills that will impact every aspect of your lives. *For booking, send email to:* **Info@BTPCompanies.com**.

Mentors help you excel to the next level. Built To Prosper Mentoring Program *(Leadership, Wealth, Business, and Health)* remains the most comprehensive program of its kind and a leader's best choice for exceeding their maximum goals.

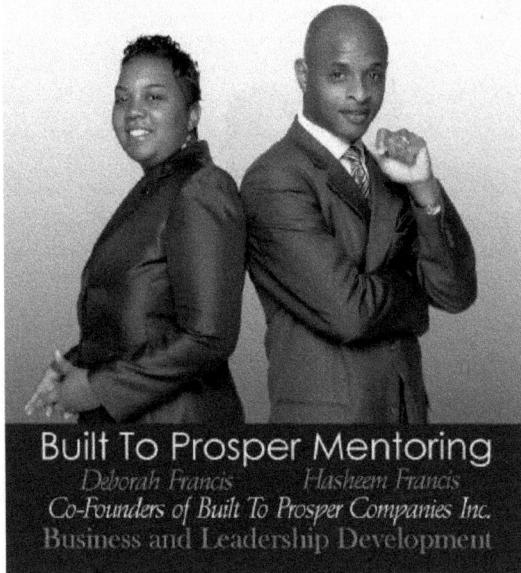

Built To Prosper Mentoring
Deborah Francis   Hasheem Francis
Co-Founders of Built To Prosper Companies Inc.
Business and Leadership Development

Our mentors specialize in giving you the latest techniques on how to become an effective leader, build a profitable business, amass wealth, and develop a healthy lifestyle. Your mentor will also instruct you on the most effective use of our proprietary materials and techniques. If you are serious about creating the life that you desire, it's time to get your own Built To Prosper Mentor. *For more information, visit: www.BTPMentoring.com.*

Built To Prosper Magazine "Created By Visionaries And Built By Leaders." **Built To Prosper Magazine** emphasizes leadership and business development; it engages and addresses every aspect of an entrepreneur's life. The magazine provides a platform for entrepreneurs to express their passion for leadership, business, family, faith, finance, and health.

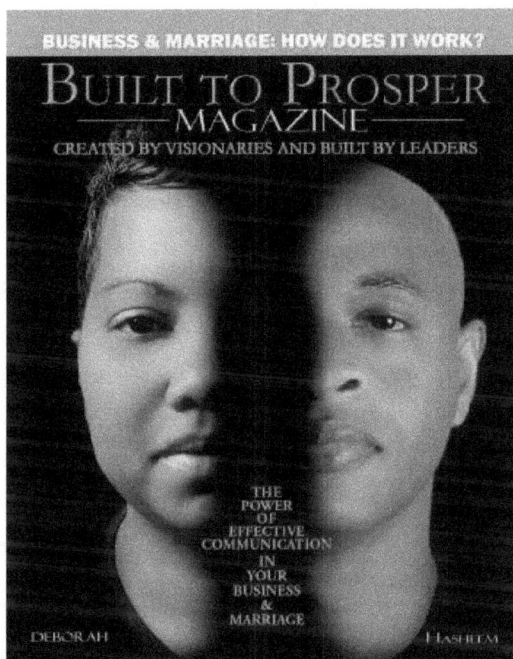

To order a copy of the fastest growing magazine, please visit: **www.BuiltToProsperMagazine.com.**

To advertise in Built To Prosper Magazine, send email to: **info@BTPCompanies.com.**

www.ingramcontent.com/pod-product-compliance
Lightning Source LLC
Chambersburg PA
CBHW071641050426
42443CB00026B/800